NOT
HERE

NOT HERE

Hieu Minh Nguyen

COFFEE HOUSE PRESS

Minneapolis

2018

Coffee House Press books are available to the trade through our primary distributor, Consortium Book Sales & Distribution, cbsd.com or (800) 283-3572. For personal orders, catalogs, or other information, write to info@coffeehousepress.org.

Coffee House Press is a nonprofit literary publishing house. Support from private foundations, corporate giving programs, government programs, and generous individuals helps make the publication of our books possible. We gratefully acknowledge their support in detail in the back of this book.

LIBRARY OF CONGRESS CATALOGING-IN-PUBLICATION DATA

Names: Nguyen, Hieu Minh, author.
Title: Not here / Hieu Minh Nguyen.
Description: Minneapolis : Coffee House Press, 2018.
Identifiers: LCCN 2017040746 | ISBN 9781566895095 (softcover : acid-free paper)
Classification: LCC PS3614.G87 A6 2018 | DDC 811/.6—dc23
LC record available at https://lccn.loc.gov/2017040746

PRINTED IN THE UNITED STATES OF AMERICA

25 24 23 22 21 20 19 18   1 2 3 4 5 6 7 8

"This is
what the living do: go in."
—*Jorie Graham*

"Let me keep on describing things to be sure they happened."
—*Jason Shinder*

Contents

**NOT
HERE**

White Boy Time Machine: Instruction Manual

In the beginning there was corn, a whole state
of boys, blond as the plants surrounding them.

:::

Oh, but why am I here?
It seems important to mention all the things

that went wrong: once, my mother loved a field & fled
from the sight of its singed face.

Once, my mother kissed my father
& the corners of his lips unraveled

& a child twice his size came out.
Once, the child cried & cried & cried

until someone put something in its mouth.

:::

Near the quarry, a population of humming
boy machines—humming love songs & the National Anthem
humming drive-in movies & pick-up trucks
humming ball caps & slow dances & pebbles at your window.

:::

I guess I'm trying to explain what's happening
                                without leaving:

I took his hand
                    & the geese came back
                                for autumn.

I bit his lip
                    & the ash spat back
                                my grandmother's bones.

I rose from his lap
                    & the dirt sunk
                                a hundred years.

I lay in his bed
                    & watched everyone
                                fall into their mothers.

                    :::

        Don't ask me how.   Don't ask if I'm a ghost.

                    :::

                            I know, I know it sounds strange
            climbing inside a boy & crawling
    out into yesterday's light.

                    :::

Somewhere somewhere
      a school of metal-clad boys.
Somewhere somewhere
      my mother is just a girl.
Somewhere somewhere
      a soldier hands her a flower
& my eyes flicker blue.

Lesson

My mother, after mistaking the rat poison

for who-knows-what, has to have her stomach filled

with charcoal. I'm always surprised how efficiently

regret can build a machine, a geared thing

charging through the narrow halls of your memory—

Asian men ain't shit, her voice a loose cork

Đàn ông của mìn không tốt & I think about my father, his temper

how she blames him for everything—*đi đi, đi đi.*

Leave. All you do is leave. For years we sat in silence

while she prayed & lit candles; asked ancestors to free me

from disease; again, blamed my father, that he taught me nothing

but desire & the desire to kill her—but still, I am surprised

when she turns to me & says, in a language I do not remember

being this soft, *Because your lover is white, you are forgiven.*

If I'm anything, I'm a boy inside his mother's body

shoveling coal into a screaming red engine.

Again, Let Me Tell You What I Know About Trust

—not a damn thing. So let me tell you what I know
about forgiveness—this joke can go on & on, see?
    I guess I'm trying to understand what makes a man
carry guilt the same way he would a bat. How my father
        after being confronted about cheating
slapped my mother, came to my room, threw my sleeping body
        over his shoulder, & drove off. Who wouldn't
beg for a story like this? A story to point & run toward
        when asked to explain every decision you've ever made
regarding love. A story to blame when your hands rush
        toward the exit. Till this day every headlight is a lullaby.
Imagine: waking up, but this time it isn't your father
        in the driver's seat, but a man who holds your head
to his lap until your breath is a song pulled from his skin
        how just like your father, even when you begged
wouldn't take you home, not until he was ready to be alone.

Still, Somehow

As boys, your father fed us fresh meat
from the lake, taught us to spit
bones into the fire, handed us each a knife
told us to enter the woods & return with something dead
& when we returned with nothing but our bodies
he assumed we failed, but what did he know about death
that we couldn't learn, will learn from our own hands
& because you aren't here (won't ever, again, be here)
to cover my mouth, I'll confess, out loud, my love, so maybe
perhaps, you will hear me & join me, here, where the sun is sweet
against the water & because I love you, I will gut this distance
with nostalgia, because grief can taste of sugar if you run
your tongue along the right edge, so let me call your name
or rather mouth it, like when we watched your father strike a cleaver
into the neck of a hawk & fell silent, not because of the blood
but rather for the way the hawk's severed body
took flight, leaving behind its head, a scarlet burden in the soil
& I wish, so badly, I was brave enough then, to keep it
to tuck it beneath my tongue for these twenty years
because darling, before I became alive, I watched the world
without knowing what to look for, but I swear, it was there, again
above the tall grass, the headless hawk
still alive, still, somehow, flying.

Nguyễn

*"It seems you've been looking out
one window, one moment all your life"*
—Cathy Song

In the beginning: a throne, of course
                set on fire.
By who?
            A brother, maybe.
Blood, always.

:::

The origin, he once told me, is simple:
the name was a mask our ancestors hid behind
to escape retribution. After the dynasty crumbled
families across the empire unified under the name
under the fear of a flag
planted through a face.

:::

I sign my name & track its scent. It leads me
to the unmarked graves of our surnames
where I carve our initials into the stone.

H.M.N. + K.T.N.

:::

Asked by the parking lot boys
who chucked rocks at our heads

if we were brothers. *Sort of,* he'd laugh.
    Our blood indistinguishable

on pavement.

                    :::

It was simple before: I could not love him

because he was a boy. I held his face

too close to mine. I hid

with our longing, underneath his bed.

When his father caught us, two flies drowning

in a dish of honey, he dragged us

onto the porch. Made us lie there

while he urinated on our backs.

                    :::

Hear a song about love found in war.
    Heat of the Madame, madame—
Miss, miss. Vision in lantern light.
    Hear a song about a soldier
about the men who've come to save her.
    Hear a song about a child

with red lips. Opium poppies
    pinned in her hair.

            :::

        I fled & did not return.
        My mother crying on the telephone

        Thank you for not killing my son.
        Sent away to live in California

        with his aunt. No good-bye, just a note
        I cannot love you, if I love you, I will die.

        For years I chose death.

            :::

        For years I refused to choose a bride.
    My mother, persistent, leaving letters

        & postcards on my pillow.
    These women will love you.

        Don't you understand? People will kill you.
    Your uncles, your father.

        My defiance soiling the lace-
    white landscape of her desires.

            :::

What was I then if not my name?

A child   of redacted blood.

& sure, I belong   to history.

I belong   to my mother's fear.

:::

He got married, she reminds me.
Why can't you?

:::

Pay attention, it's simple: *Bé Mỹ* is what
they named the children born in brothels to
American soldiers. My aunt, *Baby America,*
granted refuge by her name was my family's
greatest chance at a future. & isn't that how
we're taught to survive? Hide? Or obediently
follow the path paved by a white man's desire?

:::

Made curious by loneliness, my mother asks, without looking away
from the television, about my new lover, *her* family, if they approve of me.
Boy—friend, I remind her. The word darkening the room. & because I am now
a more brave & spiteful child, I shine my lover's photo in her face.
I wanted tears, but instead she veers off-script: *Mỹ trắng?* Her sudden smile
opening the curtains. A chorus of soldiers raises their glasses in celebration.

:::

For years I craved the red
       shock of her anger.

What do you do with tenderness
       when all you expect is fury?

He looks like he will keep you safe.
       From what? From who?

:::

It was simple before: I could not love him.

But now—

he will keep you safe.

& suddenly, the logic is gone.

Suddenly

I'm given the simple conditions

to my mother's compromise.

:::

safe.

:::

Somewhere between Saigon & Sacramento

she would sing my favorite song

if I just waved

my lover's white skin

like a flag in surrender.

:::

O, bloodless brothers
loneliness is not my only defense
                    for betrayal.

O, descendants of exile
descendants of flight
                    enough already!

Forfeit my name
if all it has offered is the curse
                    of distance.

:::

        The boy I love
        has a beautiful voice.
        Here to rescue me
        from this tragic opera.
        I, damsel spinning in the sunset.
        I, cotton candy effigy
        lighting the stage.
        How could I not
        fall for the blue-eyed hero?

With him beside me
the world is free from suffering
the bucktooth ballad
of my longing.

:::

Let me be clear: any love I find will be treason.

:::

Beloved

if what I want
more than anything
is absolution, why do I insist
on a different future?
In my dreams: I am foolish
holding a torch to a block of ice.
I think we were there, he & I
beneath it. I think we survived.

:::

In my dreams: the bouquet
falls from the sky.

Sometimes it's on fire.
Sometimes it's just a skull

but I catch it—
I catch it, every time.

Elegy for the First

Our family never understood why you never married
          why you didn't have children.
Mother, going on & on about her friends at bingo
who could've used a man   like you
       around the house.
I ask her about the man in the front row—
             the roommate, she says.   Instead
of the diagnosis,   instead of explaining
how or why, isn't it enough to say:
          no more?   Who has time
for better dreams than these? Pray for a miracle
or a good night's sleep, won't you?   Pray
       for the right ghosts   to walk you
to the end of each season.
            Uncle, a story before you sleep:
here, a child   dressed in dust.
            This time you wait for him
before you leave.   Here, another:
once, I ran, face first, into a mirror
            because I didn't recognize
my reflection, because I didn't see a reflection at all.
      I feel each shard   open me
as I walk toward you & that man, standing beside
       your open casket. He is there
               in every photograph
of you smiling.   I want to kiss him.
      I want to take him into me, soften his grief
with my heat   & inherit
any pulse you might've left behind.   *I'm sorry*
     for your loss   I say   or he says
        or neither of us say, I'm not sure.
I have so many questions. I trace
       your mouth counterclockwise
but   you do not answer.

White Boy Time Machine: Software

why did you bring me here? / i ask / the machine / has a machine family / who
assumes i've rigged their boy / to do what i want / by feeding him / a coin /
fashioned with a string / a yo-yo organ / is what the doctors called it / when
my grandmother's heart fell out of place / & did not / return to its country
whole / but who ever does / after leaving / the dinner where his parents tick-
ticked boring questions at me / *but where are you really from?* /
yesterday is the wrong answer, tomorrow too / despite memory, i believe /
in hunger / as a way to pass the time / i count the hornets that escape their
mouths / for years i lay there & pressed / an ear against the humming / the
humming i once mistook for just static / until the stingers / rose from metal
water i hear my skin sing / in a frequency made only from laughter / when
told *you speak so well* / an aubade that calls to me like a grandfather / clock
/ the machine reassures me that i have nothing / to prove / i am who they
think i am / i lace the corset, tight / blend a decimated village into the hol-
lows / of my cheeks / a dirt burlesque / a virus that breached a fire / wall of
family portraits / darkening before the embers / tear through / my future / a
year composed of bleached wires / where the rain clouds travel back & forth
/ on a clothesline / i hang his skin / to dry / i laid / his organs on a bed of rice

Type II

Ignoring the doctor's red call
        I swam in the molasses-thick swamp
    of my indulgence, allowed the sugar to ruin

the picnic. The lawn beneath me humming
        with little invaders.
    There are conditions if one insists

on knowing the secrets of my blood.
        I know it's hard to gaze at the night sky
    speckled white & not wish upon

the dead light, but I ask only for your laughter.
        I ask for all the ways I can remain
    whole & not a vision with missing limbs.

Look at the trees blistering with sap. Goddamnit
        look at me! Look at me in the old way
    in this new light.

Once I loved a boy who feared so much
        his own sickness
    I never confessed to him my own.

Afraid he would turn, with his worry, my smile
        into a knife—into a scythe
    covered in ants.

Attending the Party

To justify another month of solitude
     I tell myself, despite
my instinct to stay inside
it'll be good to exhaust myself
of the world.
       Outside
the yellow house on Portland Avenue
I kick the slush from my boots
ascending the empty porch.
       Even if I'm wrong
& the light beyond
the door is a light to nowhere
I can still say I tried, at least
      for a moment, to live
outside the warm parameters
of my loneliness. I can't stop thinking
of the old man
      who'd salt & shovel
his walk, clean & precise
every morning & how the neighbors
growing suspicious
      of the jagged terrain
of his driveway, discovered
weeks later, he'd passed away
in his sleep.
      But here is a world
where the people I love gather
in small rooms with not enough chairs.
How lucky I am
     to be missed
by those who have run out
of ways to hold me?
& isn't that what I always wanted?
      To keep something perfect
long enough for everyone to notice
when I'm gone.

Dear X

Sometimes when I wake up & my body does
not follow, I imagine it is busy lying beside
you on the hillside above the McDonough
baseball field, where the sounds from the
interstate fill the empty bleachers until
each *woosh* & horn is a father cheering
behind the chain-link backstop. I imagine
what you would say to me now if I told you
everything:

Andrew is an EMT, Kayla is a nurse, Matthew
is buff & does acid, Michael's teeth finally
grew back, Mai & Emily & Justice are all
mothers & still hate each other.

I imagine the *holy shit,* the *no way,* the *some
things never change.* I imagine the words I've
learned for us both, spoken with your boy
voice. & of course I imagine you better than
you were (happier, even), but you deserve
that. You deserve an ironed shirt. You
deserve new shoes. I describe your funeral
like a party you forgot to attend. It wasn't
the same without you.

:::

I imagine what you would say to me now if I
told you what really happened: the teacher,
my naked shape molting green in her hands,
how she would find me at Champ's play-
ground. Even in the summer. But you loved
her. You would stand on top of the hill &
wait for her car to round the corner. She'd

bring us snow cones. She'd wipe my mouth with the hem of her skirt. Sometimes, when I hate you for leaving, I wonder (& please forgive me) why she didn't choose you. She must have known. I imagine her image shattered with the same brick you tossed at Mr. Leroy's truck. I imagine the school flattened by your laughter. I imagine us slow dancing in the gymnasium with a gas can & a cigarette.

:::

One more thing before you leave: once, I chose a man because he looked how I imagine you would now. Soft hair & a flat smile. I asked him not to speak. I asked him to slap me.

What am I supposed to do now, now that I've spent most of my life without you, but still need you to save me?

As the man was leaving, I thanked him, but it wasn't for what he assumed. How could he have known? He gave me a body I did not know I missed. He gave me a body I bring with me to the hillside & lay out in the sun.

The Study

For the longest time, the only memories I had
of that year were of Little Billy from the third floor, floating
dead in the pool & how angry the rest of the tenants were
when they drained & filled it with cement
& how that summer, the unbearable heat dragged its endless skin
across our bones—memory is the funniest character in this story:
when I think of that year, no one has a face—the first memory
I had of being molested did not come until nine years later.
At first I thought it was a dream, a movie, white noise
summoning a narrative through the static—if it's true
what they say about memory being a series of rooms
then behind some locked door: a wicked apothecary: her fingers
trapped in jars, her hair growing like wild vines along the walls.
Somewhere in this story I am nine years old
filling the loud hollows with cement to drown out the ghost.
They say, *give us details,* so I give them my body.
They say, *give us proof,* so I give them my body.
If you cut me open, if you dissect me, you will pull from me:
a pair of handprints, a nine-year-old boy, fossilized.

White Boy Time Machine: Joy Ride

I go back, only to find the rest of the woman.
Her hands, stowed away. Daemons. Always with me.
Always tracing my gums. Even when I sleep—
especially when I sleep, they're there
tapping my teeth. It is the machine that pulls me
into the old elementary school
by my collar. *Heal. You need to heal.*
It is the machine that leads me
through the halls, tracking her scent.
Walls of glass. Walls of skin stretched
till translucent—except, of course, her office.
Opaque organ in a ghost body. A shadow
pacing back & forth under the door.
I want to be a braver kind of meat
to say, *show yourself* & mean it
but how long have I prepared for the dragon
only to run in the other direction. I need to explain
why. It's important that I talk about her hands
again—don't be silly. I don't love them
but I have cared for them—trimming the nails
polishing each chipped tile, just so they stay the same.
I need them to stay the same. Maybe if I bring them
to her unchanged, she'll take them back.
Maybe if I learn her face, each digit will disappear.
If I open this door, if I fill the empty spaces
if the hands leave & become a body
if I stop it from happening
who will I be on the other side?

Again, What Do I Know About Desire?

Let me explain how nothing ever changes—the scenery, sure
but everything else is the same: you take off your clothes
& become nothing, a log too wet to throw into a fire.
Ignore me. I'm still trying to figure out what it means to stay.
Us faggots are predictable this way, even when we're here
we're gone—let me explain again: he sticks a finger in my mouth
& asks me to take the ring off with my teeth & I do. I imagine
his wife's naked frame: average & angry on my tongue. I roll her
around, store her in my cheek while I suck his cock. With a chisel
she makes a statue from each tooth. Here, a dolphin. Here
a strange bird—I want to be a bird, or forgiven. It's all
very predictable. You walk into the field expecting to be
devoured & then you are. The moon, a paper plate thinning
from your sopping shape. It's all very boring, really. It ends
how it begins: a man holds out his hand & you empty
the contents of your ordinary mouth.

Cockfight

I met my brother once
in a small village in Vietnam
who, upon meeting me
grabbed my small arm
& dragged me into the woods
behind his house
where a group of men
all wearing our father's face
stood in a circle, cheering
while the two roosters
whose beaks had barbed hooks
taped to them, pecked
& clawed each other open
until the mess of bloodied feathers
were replaced by two clean birds
one, my brother's, the other
a man's, who I am told is deaf
but vicious. He told me
our father calls him long distance
from America, every week.
I can't help but wonder how
they tell the bloody roosters apart.
I told him how our father, who lives
only three miles away from me
avoids eye contact at supermarkets.
I can tell this made him happy.
Though, he didn't cheer
when the crowd cheered, when one rooster
fell to the dirt with a gash in its neck.
I knew he was the winner
when he lowered his head to hide
his smile, how he looked at me
then snatched his earnings
from the vicious man's hands.
I learned what it was like to be a brother
by watching the roosters

& how, at first, the air was calm
until they were introduced
& then they knew:
there could only be one.

#2

It's not bad luck to name your goldfish
after the goldfish that has already died

right? It seems impossible, on days like this
to walk to work & not daydream

of ways to make eye contact
with people wearing sunglasses.

It usually involves tripping or love.
My mother never told me the *no glove* rule

just hung photographs of dead relatives
in the living room & photos of herself

in my bedroom. One day, if I'm lucky
enough to outlive her, I will pick the photo

of her with the perm—she fears this the most—
that & having a son ruined by want

by the endless limbs of other sons.
My mother never told me about the first boy

I was named after—just said he died
in a desert, just said he lost his way.

She flushed my old body down the toilet
then took my photo off the wall.

Again, Let Me Explain Again

—perhaps I do want children
for reasons other than to appease my mother

give me a boy, a real boy this time, she says
either to me, or the chain of incense smoke

thinning into the realm where my grandmother sits
chewing on betel leaf, her teeth stained black

& I'm sure it's not, but maybe my mother's desire
for grandchildren has something to do with lineage

or maybe it has something to do with regret & how
for the longest time, she knelt in front of a shrine & asked

to be blessed with a daughter & here I am: the wrong
monster; truck stop prom queen in his dirt gown.

I think: If I had the answers I could answer
but I don't—I only have a number to a man

who will come, hopefully, in the next hour
to pin me to a map of hunger, stick his knuckles

into my mouth & call me his *sweet boy*

:::

Sometimes I think I could be a good father
if I don't consider myself.

How can I love something that isn't ruined?
Y'know most parents want the best for their children

& I'm sure I would too, if the child were real
but he isn't.

Each morning I send him to walk the durian orchard.
Each morning he climbs the tallest tree, picks the ripest one

& carries it home to me. The fruit's spikes sinking
into his bare arms. Each day, when he returns

he is covered in holes. I stick a coin in each one
& send him back out for milk.

:::

—c'mere darling   c'mere my darling boy   my pride & joy

—mama'slittlemama'slittle   you'll always be my, always be my

               —I always wanted alittleAsianchild

—never too old for a kiss   you're too young to know
                                    what you want

—suchalovely young   pumpkinpie   appleseed stuck in my eye

—that's my boy   oh how you've grown

               —keepyourvoicedown!

—don'tyaknow   mamaknows

        —what your mama don'tknowwon'thurt won't hurt won't hurt

—it'sokayhoney it'sokay   c'mere   come here   & let it all out

        :::

Once, I thought I saw her on the street.
You know who I'm talking about, *her.*
Though her face was still a slab of light
I was certain—something about her shadow
casting itself onto her, not like a shadow at all
more like a coat, a cold thin-blue skin
& then, I promise you, I saw her again at the grocery store
she was taller this time, much younger
something about her fingers, the rhythm
she drummed on each shelf she walked past. My pulse?
Somewhere in my dreaming I allowed this
to happen. Somewhere in that dimming landscape
me & everyone who has touched my body
gather to talk about my body.
Of course, they mention the obvious things:
a map to nowhere, a spinning blade
of wheat caught in the teeth of white men
—I swear she was there, across the pit of fire, a mask
of flames, whittling my face into a piece of wood.

:::

—attaboy —ay!boy goodjob-buddy ol'pal ol'chip-off-the-ol'

—likefatherlike sonofagun-bang-bang-pop-pop

   —hey!batterbatter hey!batterbatter-how old are you?

—hey bartender, lemme getanother-getanother

—good ol'boy from the sky-good ol'boy from the far east
        show me what the Midwest did to that rice-blood.

—waytogoCharlie! That's how you do it. That's how you shine
    like a rocket. That's how you get all the ladies.
    Spit out the dip tucked behind your lips
    & let daddy teach you how it feels to win.

    :::

—the child, too, like all dead things
is an offspring of touch.

The child hates me, but who could blame him.
We sit in silence, across from each other

at the dinner table, stripping wires
from old alarm clocks with our teeth.

Like all agony, there are pleasant moments
but only when we forget

what carried us here.
& in those moments I catch myself

being a desperate father, asking the boy
who looks too much like me

to be me, what he wants
what will make him less miserable

anything, anything you want & it's yours
usually it's nothing, some sunlight, maybe

but this time he takes a knife, runs
the blade across my stomach

& calls forth his siblings.

:::

Sometimes it's just a spider crawling up my leg
& not a hand, or the thin edge of a flame
that wakes me, or sometimes it's my mother
on the other side of the city, talking loudly
on the phone, *I think my boy is sick* & I want to be better
at lying, or at least, for heaven's sake, feel a strand
of hair graze my arm without the world around me
turning into an empty classroom, an endless row
of desks, a woman swaying at the end, her face pressed
against the chalkboard, but let me start the story over
for someone once told me that "touch" is too soft
a word to describe what happened to me & maybe
they're right, so maybe it started earlier, the woman
spending her whole life without hands, an egg
at the end of each wrist, so let's say that's true
let's say the eggs hatched & found the closest thing
to call home & here I am, today, years later, the host
of touch, a boy who lets the spider crawl onto his face
before smacking it dead.

        :::

—the children, there are thousands
now, in order not to wake me
take turns dropping a single grain of sand
onto my bed. They do this for hours, days
lost in a valley of rot.

:::

I'm afraid
if I say it out loud
I will cast a curse.
People
I'm not sure who
but people
who are smarter
than me, talk
about a circle
—a circle
of violence, or
a violent circle
or a birthday cake
with a child's face
or a carousel
of hands
or a castle
of hands, an entire
mountain, maybe.
I'm told to be open
to the possibility
of not being
a monster, not a thing
rummaged
from under a bed.
Who knows?
Some spells take years
to cast. Some men
don't know
they're hungry
until they eat.

White Boy Time Machine: Return Policy

I know it's cruel, but it's history
                the machine will say
as he holds you
          by the wrist, pulling you
                away from yesterday.
History, a velvet rope
                coiling around
your grandmother's throat.
                   You must
first wash your hands
           before flipping through
                the channels
of grief.
           You must wear the costume
                of fog, or rock
a starving child
                  to sleep
before you eat.
                 You must eat.
You must run
              in the other direction
                when time calls
       & here he is
calling your name
           like a hungry bitch
& most days you are
              a hungry bitch
so you come.
          To face the horizon
is to face today
is to turn your back on the legion of smoke
           that gave you your good name
but what can you do
             with an ocean
of singed hair
made to drag you

back to shore? If you want to feel heroic
    try balancing
        a teacup & saucer
on your head
    untying impossible
knots
        —ordinary triumphs.
Sometimes, to avoid
        a catastrophe:
the disappearance
of a limb
    or relative, you must
make sure everything burns.

Baptism

Convinced she's in hell

my mother wakes me & begs to be taken

to the lake. Wailing in prayer on the kitchen floor

her skin itching with heat, a flame seizing for god.

I believe her. One day, we will all know when suffering comes

to play the instrument of our bodies. Her song, a single note

a copper kettle whistling for mercy. From the blue-black sand

of McCarrons, I watch her disappear

under the night water. Moonlit rings

spill from her absence.

Apology, Sort Of

since the older boys agreed
to watch over me for the night
my mother, who says, *no girls no girls*
will allow me to sleep over
at my cousin's house, where the boys
in their loose shorts will take turns
standing above the air vent. The fabric
billowing & rising above their thighs
leg hairs thickening in summer.
I was an ordinary magician: pulling
something red-eyed & shaking
from ordinary cloth, while the boys
whose bodies were buoyant in darkness
peeled back their skin & showed me
how to drain the blood from a limb
how to borrow a palm from the air
to drag a hand, thick with static
under a waistband. They taught me
how to haunt my own skin—turns out
boys scare easily when softened.
Okay. I get it. There are rules
you have to follow if you want to survive.
So maybe I believed the briefs decorating
the floor were white flags I could tuck
into my pocket. Okay. So my eyes lingered
a little too long on the oldest boy
whose name became a knot in my throat
who smiled in my direction
when he emptied himself—I know. I know
you're not supposed to smile back.

Probe

In a movie I have never seen: a small-town drunk

stumbles into a beam of light & wakes up convinced

he was abducted by aliens, convinced a hole opened in the sky

& swallowed him—said they did something strange to his body

some kind of experiment, said a hole opened, said cold light

cauterized him shut, redefined that red theory, chrome instrument

turned him into a skinless puzzle, a scrambled egg

sealed back into its shell. Madness, too, can be cumulative.

When my blood seemed uncontrollable, ran messy with pulp

down their fingers, my cousins finally left the room, laughing

closing the basement door behind them.

Punish

The last time I wet the bed
my mother pulled off my pants
pinned my face to the sopping mattress
& threatened me with needle & thread.

I'm trying to understand that memory
is not a technology, a full charge
will get you nowhere, if you're stuck
tracing the perimeters of your dull nostalgia
for an exit. My hands clutch a wheel
attached to nothing.

I'm often asked why I left my mother
her old age scaling the high-rise of her spine.

Listen, trying to forget is not the same
as leaving—sometimes we must
forget to allow forgiveness
to comb the knots from our hair.

I'm sure it's wrong, but I have this theory:
at the root of all of our sorrow there's a woman
taking a long sip of water.

Mercy

Once, while lying in his bed

      a man asked me to quiet

his dog by speaking to it

      in Vietnamese, said

well, she is your people

      & if you need to inquire

about the breed

      we cannot drink

from the same glass

      & I am telling you this

not because I trust you

      but because I truly wanted

to ignore him, to close my eyes

      & let my mouth fill

with his spit, but that wreckage

      was a wall too thin

to fuck against—I hear what you're

      saying, *mercy mercy*

lighten up & I think about all the men

    who've touched my body

& which of them own dogs

    & which of them I could see

making this joke, or finding it funny

    & I know, I know

I'm being unreasonable—there was a time

    I would have stayed

& watched the trees fall all around me.

    There was a time

I wouldn't have made a sound

    while the fire traced my erection.

Yes. I'm calling it a fire.

    You should too.

Wherever he laid his hands

    hair singed down to the skin.

I really should get a sense of humor

    but that requires enduring

the labor of forgetting. Look here, I'm tired

    of pretending the room

isn't halfway ash, or filling with a smoke

    so thick I mistake it

for the tips of his fingers. Ready at the socket

    to gift me a new kind

of longing. Won't you do this for me?

    Switch beds with me—

just for the night, just to see how hard it is

    to sleep when all you hear

is laughter.

White Boy Time Machine: Safety Tips

i understand no one / wants to be remembered / at their twenty-year high school reunion / as the guy who cut off the tips of his fingers / trying to dissect a fetal pig / i really wish i could help / everyone / who asked / for winning lottery numbers / or a second chance / at something better / than a fully furnished patio / but no matter how many times i've tried / the town still burns / unlike a wound / or fire, time needs no tending / 'cause the flames will come / even if they don't come / from your hands / *are we done here* / the machine asks, while buttoning its pants / the red metal / of its hips / cooling / near a river / i see my grandfather / for the first time / he is not a photograph / i want to fall into / his hands / my favorite story / begins with / *let me remember* / i cannot / stop him from disappearing / into the wall / of smoke / i don't know / how much ruin / i can drag through time / how much ash can fill / a bed before history / claims my name / let me tell you the problem / with history / somewhere somewhere someone wants you / gone / don't you think i know / the rules / fasten your seat belt / keep your arms inside / the white boy's throat / a light jacket for the rain

B.F.F.

I lie in the dark & stretch the portrait
of a white woman across my face
until it splits. Beneath my bed, a catalog
of half-faced women sing me to sleep.
I'll start with Amanda Elias
& how I thought, in order to be worthy
of desire, I had to wear her skin.
For four years I sat across from her
in the lunchroom, mimicked her posture
blinked when she did, became the mirror
so concerned with the rise & fall
of each one of her blemishes
I even took her to the winter formal
watched, in the green glow of the gymnasium
at how I—she danced, chiffon willow
silk mystic. I watched how the boys held her
whispered a joke in her ear that made me laugh.
Stupid boys. Stupidstupid boys.
I tell the man in the chatroom
I am a platter of soft curls. Send him her photo.
Crack an egg & remove the yolk.
He could marry me, you know? You don't.
She would never. Once, after another heartbreak
she came to school with cuts on her wrist
& maybe my rage was out of concern—I was
after all, a great friend, unflinching in my kindness
or maybe I hated how ungrateful she was
or maybe I thought her technique was pathetic
horizontal, barely breaking the first layer
or maybe I wanted a bigger opening
to attach a zipper, slip on her hand-me-downs
& somehow she must've known all along
her body was a dress I hung for motivation
the way she cried while I held her wrist
dabbing it with cold water, inspecting the damage
how she kept on saying, *Sorry. Sorry.*

Pig

You were once & perhaps continue to be

the myth you tell to scare yourself

into loneliness. Copper totem rusting blue

in your throat. Once, a man paid

to watch you eat. There are countless ways

to justify company. Hunger, overdue balance, whatever.

Cartoon savage licking the throne clean.

& isn't that what you always wanted?

To be filled & emptied? To bite the hand

that feeds you? Even if the hand wants to be bitten?

& is that defiance? Standing naked

at a dinner table while oil drips

from your chin, wanting the man

to touch you, but he won't. & you want

to be the kind of person who doesn't need

to feel beautiful, but you are. You are

predictable in your longing. Grotesque muse

spinning marrow into lace. Spit bride

glistening beneath a chandelier

stunning, even just for a moment.

Hosting

Because I didn't want to do anything
      I got on my knees & offered him
the easy currency of my mouth—
      I don't want to explain a thing
but if I have to, I want to make clear
      I knew, if I just asked him to leave
he would have, but I didn't want him
      to come all that way for nothing.
He showed up & that meant something
      I think. Who am I to care?
Who am I to turn away anything as simple
      as hunger? What is my body
if not wet collateral? & then he said
      I can't get off on just head
so I let him fuck me facedown on the carpet
      while I counted the loose
change under the dresser & that only
      feels important to mention
because later I used it to buy him a sandwich
      I don't think he even touched.

:::

I've learned quickly, there are countless ways to open
a carcass. Silence is one. I can't say for sure
but I think I'm bored with loneliness
or at least the music it supplies: bodies thrashing.
It's harder than it looks. Opening & closing.
Doing whatever it takes to pull that bright crescendo
into the humming dark. I imagine my hands: wreckless
running up & down his cock, a pair of scissors
curling the ribbon of his blood.

:::

Dumb, I know, but still, I let the strange man spend the night.
I know his type. He won't do anything unless I ask. So I ask.

All I've ever wanted to be was useful. I can't stop talking about desire.
I used to think of it as a pane of glass I would press my face against

& then one day it came, one day I fell through
the glass or the boy or the men in their many faces

until I was just a thin coat of leather on everyone's teeth.

:::

Listen, I understand there's still time to be saved
                there's always someone waiting to name your story.
        Shut up! I know the story, or at least the lesson:

the hand, the stove top—except I'm not sure
if I'm the hand or stove. Maybe I'm looking at it
                all wrong. Maybe I should admit I do know
what I'm doing. He'll leave soon & I'll be just fine.

I'll be just fine.

:::

The man wakes me up by slipping a finger inside.

I don't move away, can't go back to sleep

until he's done. It would be too easy

to make him leave, to roll on my back

to scream out the open window, but instead

I laugh & say, *you won't find it—you won't*

find whatever you're looking for.

White Boy Time Machine: Override

No matter where we go, there's a history
of white men describing a landscape

so they can claim it. I look out the window
& I don't see a sunset, I see a man's

pink tongue razing the horizon.
I once heard a man describe the village

in Vietnam where my family comes from.
It was beautiful

a poem I would gift my mother
but somewhere in the pastoral I am reminded

a child (recently) was blown apart
after stepping on a mine, a bulb, I guess

blooming forty years later—
maybe it was how the poet said *dirt*

or maybe it was how he used fire
to describe the trees.

Changeling

Standing in front of a mirror, my mother tells me she is ugly
says the medication is making her fat. I laugh & walk her
back to bed. My mother tells me she is ugly in the same voice
she used to say *no woman could love you* & I watch her
pull at her body & it is mine. My heavy breast.
My disappointing shape. She asks for a bowl of plain broth
& it becomes the cup of vinegar she would pour down my throat.
Every day after school, I would kneel before her.
I would remove my clothes & ask her to mark the progress.
It's important that I mention, I truly wanted to be beautiful
for her. In my dreams I am thin & if not thin, something better.
I tell my mother she is still beautiful & she laughs. The room fills
with flies. They gather in the shape of a small boy. They lead her
back to the mirror, but my reflection is still there.

Commute

Would I be
a decent exorcist
running a braid
of copper wires
along my mother's
teeth to see
the flames
change colors?
Her hands
sometimes small
as coins, reach
for me, even
when the moths
make up most
of my anatomy.
I know she's sorry
for the bad years:
I packed my bags
once. I slept in
a neighbor's car once.
I know it's cruel
to make her
wear the same dress
in every memory
to say *forgive*
yet stitch a mask
on her while she sleeps.
I always knew
guilt would keep her
from noticing
the money missing
from under her
mattress.
I could get away
with being clumsy
with knives.

Every surface
punctured.
Every curtain
drawn. The house
still sinking
when no one is
on board.
It beckons me
from the highway
to watch
the one lit room
slowly go dark.
I want to break
its windows
with my face.

Ode to the Pubic Hair Stuck in My Throat

O diligent survivor
        clinging
to the edge
of a chasm.

Little tickle.
        Little wire
        picking open
the doors
illuminating the corners
of my mouth
I did not know
could swell with touch.

Bless touch, I guess
its round noise.

O little brown figure
        coiling
in the middle
of that soft pink
alley
        how lonely
        it must be
to come from desire
        but end
        where light ends.

Son of the floorless
        prayer
son of the O horizon
remind me
what it's like to speak
without
        a white man
flickering in my throat.

O small equator
        making
every story
a ruined portrait.
Bless the fault line

beyond my reach
        little fracture
in my speech.
Little secret

        I keep
trying to cough up
but instead
cause my mother
        to raise
her small hands
to my forehead.
        Con nóng?

        Bless also
my mother
her perfect temperature
her concern
the only language
        we have
to say
sorry.

Bless language
its impossible walls
its flexible agony
        a thin line
I keep tripping over.

O little thread
undoing
        the hem
of my body—

but wait, bless also
      my body
how it rejects
the unfamiliar
      convulsing
      conversing
with itself
      excising
      evicting
      cutting down
the rope
bridge
      rolling
the debris
into a question
mark on my tongue.

Note

It's important to mention
the only time my mother speaks
in English is when I make her speak
in a poem. So she says, *get out*—says, *leave*
but it's me, my voice, that slams the door.
The only way out is through the opening
of her mouth. *The only way toward salvation
is forgiveness,* the aunts would say, licking their thumbs
to cross my forehead. Sure, the only mask I own
is humming on my face. I want to study
the mechanics of leaving. Go. Go! Go so I can see.
Slow so I can watch everything fade to water.
I think it was Sappho who said, *I long & seek after*
but of course, that's not what she said, not exactly.

Politics of an Elegy

in conversation with Danez Smith & Sam Sax

If things happen
the way they are supposed to
my mother will die before me.
My mother, who, by then, will love me
will die.

My mother, who, by then
will, hopefully, be happy, will walk
without pain from this life into the next

& I, her only son, her writer son
will stay to translate
her life into English.

Any adjective can be true
if you cry hard enough.

I can lie & say I haven't written the poem
haven't buried her over & over at my desk
haven't described the ash of her body.

I throw a fist full of sand in the air
& pretend to weep.

I write the poem.
I fill my lungs with English.
I numb her skin with English.
I English the light she walks into.

I kill her
just to raise her from the dead.

I anticipate this grief by exhausting it
with music. I pry open the casket.
I make her twirl in the center.

White Boy Time Machine: Error

the machine scans the images of the dead / into the glowing flatbed / of his chest / & still my grief / is a foreign currency / he spits out / synthesized birds fly hollow / out of the jukebox / women cry in a pitch mistaken for music / there is a language missing / in the stainless steel interior of our love / i see little futures in the distance, but none belong / with him / there is breakfast in the morning & dinner / at night he enters me / & sure, it is me sometimes, my body / that turns on / a projector in my mouth / on the side of the barn / we watch a car / a village / a church / flatten / the file into / a disc fractured / after the cops beat my cousin / for months he would / *lie in bed all day with me* / kiss me again so i can see / my empty / home in the glitching sky beyond / the caution tape / police cars flash / blue / in the machine's eye / a telescope / i cannot focus / with him beside me / i am beginning to forget what to expect from the world i always knew / i would have to leave / everyone including my mother / adores him / i understand / maybe / i'm scared / i tell him / *of what?* / he asks / *of who?*

The Ranger

In the movie the musical the play   the opera
the white soldier leaves   & the brown beauty kills herself
on stage   on screen   on Washington Street.
Dearest, darling,   pumpkin seed harlot
shimmy shimmy in your blood bodice,   your sunrise negligee—
negligee, derived from the French,   meaning, *neglected.*
Meaning, trip wire lingerie. Meaning, bandage gauze
camisole. Butcher paper   parasol opening beneath the knife.
Beneath the wife   of contrails, spelling out   *Broadway, here I come!*
He tells me the promotion means he gets to carry a gun.
My lover is gone. Replaced by a badge.   It's not a question   of *who left who?*
but rather, *how*   *could either of us stay?*   In my bed, the red dust
cratered around our final departure.   Our image spliced in half
by the blade of the horizon.   He is gone.   I am not.
Not a seam opening.   Not a good-luck appendage
to hang on a rearview mirror.   Not a ballad beckoning the curtains.
Not the end.   Not now.   Not here.

Afterwards

for RV

It already feels like a different world
                        than the one I began
holding your hand—but it's the stillness
I can't ignore.
                        You couldn't see
        the landscape changing.
If what I am
            is a postcard you send to your mother
then you are the crumpled image of a plane
                    flightless span of metal
I clutch to my chest.
        How can I say it so you know?
Everywhere we went, you held open the door
                but did not walk through.
You're doing just fine
                    you say.
You are somewhere between
                            where you are
& somewhere you'll always be:
                    you did not mean to say—
you are trying to understand that—
                    you did not mean to offend—
Me?   I am charting the distances we traveled
on a blank white map.
                        I am drawing the child
we could never have
                    & I can hear its laughter.
I can hear it speak, void of any accent.
                            Static in the air.
            It's simple, really.
You, like the other yous
are gone,   returned to the God of metals.
& if I were to forgive you (& I know I could)
who would be left
who would be left   to forgive me?

Reunion

You can't uncremate your grandmother.
You can't think of regret as a town
you move to when grief snores too loud
in every room. You can't siphon her dust
back into your arms & if you could
she'd still be gone, still be the coat of gray
settling on the windowsill. Be grateful
for the first child who dug a hole
& thought *mother*. Be grateful that we bury
our dead & not leave them where they died:
bodies flooding over highway medians; the bed you shared
& will continue to share with your grandmother;
the city, a sea of leather ruined by heat.
In death we belong to everyone
who can pass our names through their warm mouths
who can smell the rotten air without flinching
who can tilt their noses up into the sky & think *family*.

Heavy

The narrow clearing down to the river
I walk alone, out of breath

my body catching on each branch.
Small children maneuver around me.

Often, I want to return to my old body
a body I also hated, but hate less

given knowledge.
Sometimes my friends—my friends

who are always beautiful & heartbroken
look at me like they know

I will die before them.
I think the life I want

is the life I have, but how can I be sure?
There are days when I give up on my body

but not the world.
I am alive. I know this. Alive now

to see the world, to see the river
rupture everything with its light.

Monica West Is Moving to Omaha, Nebraska

Monica West takes to the stage in a dress ready to fringefuck your conservative relatives into a bathhouse. Her wig, jet black, a dance of crow feathers. Powerhouse of the Midwest, back-alley glamour sexed auntie in a pair of six-inch heels, disco ball bastard slut in the blood moon—she snaps her fingers & all the dollar bills fly from my hands. My rent, my next three meals, at the foot of her patent leather mercy—

I don't believe in psychiatrists. I don't believe in the church of therapy, but I do believe, I guess, in healing. Asclepius in a lace front Donatella. I believe my friends, who tell me they are sad, or scared, but still need to get out of the house. *Just for the night. Just for tonight.* I believe there is no shame in showing up to the club wearing sweatpants. No shame in the way the bass bounces with our scent. Glitter musk dizzying the floor. *10 p.m. every Saturday!* In Northeast Minneapolis, a drag queen streaks a beam of light across the high points of her cheeks & transports me to a new world: debutante debauchery, cock-ring cotillion—

Danez & I aren't amateurs. We know better. We make reservations. Every week, every Saturday we claim the good seats. Rookie queers stand in the back. We tell all of our friends that Vicky's got some of the best fried chicken in Minneapolis, which doesn't really mean much, considering the white folks this far north either under-spice or over-spice their food like they're overcompensating for history, for their ancestors' long legacy of trying to eradicate flavor from the entire fucking planet—

But leave it to these faggots to get it right. Spice just right. Cook just right. Look just right. Lips, eyeliner, tights just right—but we don't come here for the fried chicken. We don't come here because the white people are better here than they are in the real world, cause after all, after last call, they will all leave & walk into a world where their clean faces have been the destination in the path of our unmaking. Cause after all, *no blacks, no asians, no spice, no rice, no fats, no femmes.* They push my friends, & say *I don't see you—didn't see you standing there—*

We don't come here to fight, though we will fight. Look here, when we show up to the club, to the party, to our jobs at your worst, know, we are always ready to be our best. Show out. Show up. Show the fuck up to a country that uninvites you to the parade. Show up anyway—

Monica West announces she is moving to Omaha, Nebraska. My first thought, *why?* My second, still, *why?* But then I think about Saturday, the one after the election, or the one after the shooting, or the one the night before, or the one the night of—I think of every inevitable Saturday that will follow every inevitable tragedy. I think about the world on fire & the music we choose to play anyway. & I wonder if I will ever be brave enough to leave one day. If I will, one day, ever get out of this town, this country, this world. If sanctuary is not a place, but the people we love all under the same impossible & temporary light, how can we convince anyone to stay? How do I see this through? Goddamnit, how can I stop people from leaving—

But we don't come here for sanctuary. We know better. We come here for Monica West, for Victoria DeVille, for Kamaree Williams, for the way Kyle's ass looks tonight. We come here because I think Danez will make a great drag queen, because I see a world where the people I love sing their favorite songs. I see a world where the crowds cheer for their brown & perfect bodies. I see a world where I stay, where I stand at the foot of the stage & wait for them to reach down & take, I don't know, my money? My hand? My fear of a world that refuses to know their glory?

Notes on Staying

All my life I've watched my mother contemplate an exit, hovering between a conversation & a doorway. Her sleep, medicated & rich. I imagine in her dreams she is tall with laughter. I feel most like her son when I am lonely—a child again, dragged by her to a party I enjoyed, then stopped enjoying. In our future, there are two cabs idling in the driveway, which is a cowardly way of saying, *I cannot kill myself until my mother dies.* If joy is what tethers us to this life, then most days, my mother & I float above the pavement, tied together by the fraying threads of her nightgown. All my life I've bitten at the knots of my solitude. No one wants to be alive when they're forgotten. When she is gone, who will call my name?

I've tried my hardest to build a world, separate from
my mother, that would be hard to leave, but instead,
the water runs clear & the minnows swim, bright,
beneath it, & some big god in my big head tells me,
my son, you are not needed & the voice is soft & cruel
& all my big loves are laughing & happy & today my
body does not fit between this joy & today everything
is indescribably beautiful & it must be wrong to want
anything else because even the blaring sounds of the
city are calm & the sun laughs, *stay, not today, not today.*

I feel furthest from wanting to live when I think of joy as some kind of destination, a two-story house around the corner with a basketball hoop in the driveway, where the children (mine, I guess) take turns standing on each other's shoulders to pass the ball through the net's red mouth. I guess, by staying, I'm saying, *I want to live in this house*—but I'm not. I'm saying, *one day, I want things to be easier.* Too often, I don't tell people (people I love) I am sad. I don't think that's something they would want to hear. Because they love me. Because I don't want them to feel like the currency of their tenderness isn't enough when it has been & will be again, but, well, if I'm being completely honest, today is hard. Today I miss people. Dead & alive. Far & near. I miss them all. & I think I'm boring you & well, that doesn't feel too great.

& I should mention hope, since hope is what disarms
the bomb when the city clutches its children good-night,
the red wire blue wire optimism of my mother's voice,
when she says, *I don't need friends, just you* & in me still
a child refusing to accept the terms of her mercy & how
many times have I been told, *you'll understand when
you're older,* or how many times have I heard, *we're all
gonna die one day*—boring hopelessness, clearing the
table before we eat, which is fine, who needs a last meal?
Who needs a good reason to leave the party before
things get weird? So maybe that's hope. Maybe hope is
stopping the story before it's over, before the inevitable
messy end. O monger of the broken records. O monger
of the early birthday present. Push me from the high-
way overpass—let's leave the story there, let's leave
the body whole, in mid-air, illuminated by oncoming
headlights, a tiny song, a pixel in the pixelated mouth
of hope, or whatever it is that propels us through the
door of tomorrow & since there was no key, I guess I'll
swallow the door.

Notes

"White Boy Time Machine: Return Policy" opens with a line borrowed from the movie *Time Traveller: The Girl Who Leapt Through Time.*

"Elegy for the First" contains a line inspired by Adélia Prado's poem "Seductive Sadness Winks at Me."

"Note" was written after a conversation with Gretchen Marquette.

Acknowledgments

Many thanks to the editors of the following publications, where a number of these poems first appeared, sometimes in different versions:

The Academy of American Poets' Poem-a-Day series— "Heavy"

The Adroit Journal — "Apology, Sort Of" and "Commute"

Bat City Review — "Punish"

BOAAT — "Ode to the Pubic Hair Stuck in My Throat"

BuzzFeed — "B. F. F."

Devil's Lake — "White Boy Time Machine: Instruction Manual"

Guernica — "White Boy Time Machine: Software"

Gulf Coast — "Dear X"

HEArt Journal Online — "Mercy"

Hobart — "White Boy Time Machine: Return Policy," "Type II," "Afterwards," and "The Study"

Into Quarterly — "Attending the Party"

Nashville Review — "White Boy Time Machine: Override" and "Elegy for the First"

Nepantla — "Again, What Do I Know About Desire?"

Ninth Letter — "White Boy Time Machine: Safety Tips" and "White Boy Time Machine: Joy Ride"

The Offing — "Notes on Staying [All my life I've watched]" and "Notes on Staying [& I should mention hope]"

The Paris-American — "Cockfight" and "#2"

Pinwheel — "Hosting" and "Again, Let Me Explain Again"

POETRY — "Changeling" and "Probe"

Poetry London — "Nguyễn"

Southern Indiana Review — "Again, Let Me Tell You What I Know About Trust"

Split This Rock [Poem of the Week] — "Politics of an Elegy"

Vinyl Poetry — "Reunion"

"#2" appears in *The Dead Animal Handbook* anthology published by University of Hell Press, edited by Cam Awkward-Rich and Sam Sax.

"White Boy Time Machine: Instruction Manual" has been republished in *Bettering American Poetry* & *PBS NewsHour*.

"Cockfight" has been republished in *Inheriting the War: Poetry and Prose by Descendants of Vietnam Veterans and Refugees* (W. W. Norton, 2017).

Many, many thanks to Chris Fischbach, Caroline Casey, and the wonderfully warm and generous folks at Coffee House Press for believing in this collection. Extra shout-out to Carla Valadez!

For their support, endless encouragement, and guidance throughout the creation of this book (and my everyday life), I would like to thank the people who teach me, every day, what tenderness can supply: Sam Sax, Fatimah Asghar, Danez Smith, Paul Tran, Franny Choi, Cam Awkward-Rich, Anders Carlson-Wee, Michael Lee, Gretchen Marquette, Nghiem Tran, Sierra DeMulder—and of course, Paul Otremba, your wisdom, your patience, your kinship, carry me every day. Thank you for finding me.

My gratitude also belongs to the people who have sustained me, my friends, my peers, my teachers, my heroes, my forever people: Tish Jones, Tabia Yapp, Safia Elhillo, Ocean Vuong, Dobby Gibson, Rachel Rostad, Nate Marshall, Angel Nafis, Leigh Lucas, Amy Lin, Carlos Andrés Gómez, Mikal Goetz, Justin Phillip Reed, Jamila Woods, Monica Sok, Marci Calabretta Cancio-Bello, Hanif Abdurraqib, Jayson Smith, Cathy Linh Che, Phillip B. Williams, Kaveh Akbar, Saeed Jones, Patricia Smith, Carrie Mar, Clare Needham, Gabriel Zea, Martina Potratz, Antonius Bui, Nat Schmookler, Mong-jane Wu, Min Shu Cheng, Colleen Mullins, Fatima Camara, Donte Collins, Anessa Ibrahim, Rachel McKibbens, Shira Erlichman, Rachel Wiley, Britteney Kapri, Raych Jackson, Ariana Brown, Chen Chen, Tarfia Faizullah, Terrance Hayes, Dana Levin, Spencer Retelle, Khary Jackson, Kyle Tran Myhre, Michael Mlekoday, Yazmin Monét Watkins, Chrysanthemum

Tran, Charlotte Abotsi, Joshua Nguyen, Lauren Bullock, Kyra Calvert, Taneum Bambrick, Melissa Lozada-Oliva, Olivia Gatwood, Jeremiah Ellison, Arianna Genis, Lara Avery, Terisa Siagatonu, Esme Franklin, Amie Durenberger, Pauline Johnson, C.J. Anderson, Mandy Brown, Monica Brosi, Monica West, Victoria DeVille, Kamaree Williams, Bad Karma, Crystal Belle, Eduardo Corral, Christopher Soto, Emily Yoon, Michael Bazzett, Stevie Edwards, Sam Cook, Sarah Kay, Sarah Gambito, Joseph Legaspi, Jennifer Chang, Ellen Bryant Voigt, Debra Allbery, C. Dale Young, Matthew Olzmann, Bao Phi, Nabila Lovelace, the 2017 Conversation Fellows. Thank you for making it worth it.

Further thanks to the people, organizations, and spaces that have granted me time and space to write this book: Kundiman, TruArtSpeaks, the MFA Program for Writers at Warren Wilson College, the National Endowment for the Arts, the Minnesota State Arts Board, the Loft Literary Center, the Metropolitan Regional Arts Council, the Vermont Studio Center, the University of Arizona Poetry Center, the Miami Writers Institute, the Queens at Lush, Button Poetry.

And lastly, I thank my mom, the person I understand most in this world.

Hieu Minh Nguyen is a fiscal year 2016 recipient of an Artist Initiative grant from the Minnesota State Arts Board. This activity is made possible by the voters of Minnesota through a grant from the Minnesota State Arts Board, thanks to a legislative appropriation by the Minnesota Legislature, and by a grant from the National Endowment for the Arts.

LITERATURE
is not the same thing as
PUBLISHING

Coffee House Press began as a small letterpress operation in 1972 and has grown into an internationally renowned nonprofit publisher of literary fiction, essay, poetry, and other work that doesn't fit neatly into genre categories.

Coffee House is both a publisher and an arts organization. Through our *Books in Action* program and publications, we've become interdisciplinary collaborators and incubators for new work and audience experiences. Our vision for the future is one where a publisher is a catalyst and connector.

This project was made possible
through generous support from

THE FRINGE FOUNDATION

Funder Acknowledgments

Coffee House Press is an internationally renowned independent book publisher and arts nonprofit based in Minneapolis, MN; through its literary publications and *Books in Action* program, Coffee House acts as a catalyst and connector—between authors and readers, ideas and resources, creativity and community, inspiration and action.

Coffee House Press books are made possible through the generous support of grants and donations from corporations, state and federal grant programs, family foundations, and the many individuals who believe in the transformational power of literature. This activity is made possible by the voters of Minnesota through a Minnesota State Arts Board Operating Support grant, thanks to the legislative appropriation from the arts and cultural heritage fund. Coffee House also receives major operating support from the Amazon Literary Partnership, the Jerome Foundation, The McKnight Foundation, Target Foundation, and the National Endowment for the Arts (NEA). To find out more about how NEA grants impact individuals and communities, visit www.arts.gov.

Coffee House Press receives additional support from the Elmer L. & Eleanor J. Andersen Foundation; the David & Mary Anderson Family Foundation; the Buuck Family Foundation; Fredrikson & Byron, P.A.; Dorsey & Whitney LLP; the Fringe Foundation; Kenneth Koch Literary Estate; the Knight Foundation; the Rehael Fund of the Minneapolis Foundation; the Matching Grant Program Fund of the Minneapolis Foundation; Mr. Pancks' Fund in memory of Graham Kimpton; the Schwab Charitable Fund; Schwegman, Lundberg & Woessner, P.A.; the U.S. Bank Foundation; VSA Minnesota for the Metropolitan Regional Arts Council; and the Woessner Freeman Family Foundation in honor of Allan Kornblum.

The Publisher's Circle of Coffee House Press

Publisher's Circle members make significant contributions to Coffee House Press's annual giving campaign. Understanding that a strong financial base is necessary for the press to meet the challenges and opportunities that arise each year, this group plays a crucial part in the success of Coffee House's mission.

Recent Publisher's Circle members include many anonymous donors, Suzanne Allen, Patricia A. Beithon, the E. Thomas Binger & Rebecca Rand Fund of the Minneapolis Foundation, Robert & Gail Buuck, Claire Casey, Louise Copeland, Jane Dalrymple-Hollo, Mary Ebert & Paul Stembler, Kaywin Feldman & Jim Lutz, Chris Fischbach & Katie Dublinski, Sally French, Jocelyn Hale & Glenn Miller, the Rehael Fund-Roger Hale/Nor Hall of the Minneapolis Foundation, Randy Hartten & Ron Lotz, Dylan Hicks & Nina Hale, William Hardacker, Jeffrey Hom, Carl & Heidi Horsch, Amy L. Hubbard & Geoffrey J. Kehoe Fund, Kenneth Kahn & Susan Dicker, Stephen & Isabel Keating, Kenneth Koch Literary Estate, Cinda Kornblum, Jennifer Kwon Dobbs & Stefan Liess, Lenfestey Family Foundation, Sarah Lutman & Rob Rudolph, the Carol & Aaron Mack Charitable Fund of the Minneapolis Foundation, George & Olga Mack, Joshua Mack & Ron Warren, Gillian McCain, Mary & Malcolm McDermid, Sjur Midness & Briar Andresen, Maureen Millea Smith & Daniel Smith, Peter Nelson & Jennifer Swenson, Enrique Olivarez, Jr. & Jennifer Komar, Alan Polsky, Marc Porter & James Hennessy, Robin Preble, Alexis Scott, Ruth Stricker Dayton, Jeffrey Sugerman & Sarah Schultz, Nan G. & Stephen C. Swid, Patricia Tilton, Joanne Von Blon, Stu Wilson & Melissa Barker, Warren D. Woessner & Iris C. Freeman, Margaret Wurtele, and Wayne P. Zink & Christopher Schout.

For more information about the Publisher's Circle and other ways to support Coffee House Press books, authors, and activities, please visit www.coffeehousepress.org/support or contact us at info@coffeehousepress.org.

Hieu Minh Nguyen is the son of Vietnamese immigrants. His debut collection of poetry, *This Way to the Sugar,* was a finalist for both a Minnesota Book Award and a Lambda Literary Award. Nguyen has received awards and fellowships from the National Endowment for the Arts, Kundiman, the Vermont Studio Center, the Minnesota State Arts Board, and the Loft Literary Center. His poems have appeared in *Poetry,* the *Offing, BuzzFeed,* the Poem-a-Day series from the Academy of American Poets, and elsewhere. He lives in Minneapolis.

Not Here was designed by
Bookmobile Design & Digital Publisher Services.
Text is set in Arno Pro.